Asset Kids
How Kids Can Help Their Mom and Dad?

by:
George Razon Wu, Jr
Jaden Razon Wu

APARTMENT
PRESCRIPTION

Video link of the book

https://youtu.be/3UpagUdJmPk

This is how we spend our Sunday.

We go to church.

We inspect our apartments.

We visit our tenants.

We inspect more properties.

We help throw away garbage in our apartments.

We help shovel snow
in our apartments.

We have a business meeting
on how to grow our business.

We share what we learned about business.

Income is money you make from your business or job such as shoveling snow, helping your mom and dad in their business like throwing away garbage or making ad videos for their business.

Expense is money you pay for items like food, clothes, and toys.

Assets put money into your wallet. Examples of assets are writing books and selling them, apartments, lemonade stand.

Liabilities take money out of your wallet. Examples of liabilities are having many clothes, many toys and many candy.

We promote our business online and when we go to places like Lowes or an event or a party.

We do Math.
Income - Expense = Cashflow
7 - 2 = 5

We learned income and expense.
We learned assets and liabilities.

Process Page
LOGOTYPE
Main Title
75%
25%
65%
85%
50%
35%
Option A
Option B
Option C
Option D
Option E
Option F
Title Value
Your Title
Proin efficitur ornare turpis, vel pulvinar risus maximus nec. Lorem ipsum dolor sit amet.
Your Title
Proin efficitur ornare turpis, vel pulvinar risus maximus nec. Lorem ipsum dolor sit amet.
Your Title
Proin efficitur ornare turpis, vel pulvinar risus maximus nec. Lorem ipsum dolor sit amet.
Your Title
Proin efficitur ornare turpis, vel pulvinar risus maximus nec. Lorem ipsum dolor sit amet.
Your Title
Proin efficitur ornare turpis, vel pulvinar risus maximus nec. Lorem ipsum dolor sit amet.

We always look for ways to grow our business.

We help with household chores by fixing our bed and cleaning up our toys after we play.

We help with household chores by folding our clothes.

My brother and I
have simple fun.

My brother and
I have our own
business meeting
about making our
1st book.

Kids, how can you help your mom and dad at home?

How can you help your mom and dad with their business?

Kids, what do you love to do best?

What things can you sell online?

What products can you create to start your own business?

Family help each other
be a better person.

APARTMENT
PRESCRIPTION

Made in United States
Orlando, FL
04 November 2026

90205466R00019